T0413810

FAMOUS SHIPWRECKS
PACIFIC OCEAN SHIPWRECKS

by Michelle Parkin

po go

Ideas for Parents and Teachers

Pogo Books let children practice reading informational text while introducing them to nonfiction features such as headings, labels, sidebars, maps, and diagrams, as well as a table of contents, glossary, and index.

Carefully leveled text with a strong photo match offers early fluent readers the support they need to succeed.

Before Reading

- "Walk" through the book and point out the various nonfiction features. Ask the student what purpose each feature serves.
- Look at the glossary together. Read and discuss the words.

Read the Book

- Have the child read the book independently.
- Invite him or her to list questions that arise from reading.

After Reading

- Discuss the child's questions. Talk about how he or she might find answers to those questions.
- Prompt the child to think more. Ask: Why have ships sunk in the Pacific Ocean? What could ships have done differently to stay safe?

Pogo Books are published by Jump!
5357 Penn Avenue South
Minneapolis, MN 55419
www.jumplibrary.com

Library of Congress Cataloging-in-Publication Data is available at www.loc.gov or upon request from the publisher.

ISBN: 979-8-88996-668-5 (hardcover)
ISBN: 979-8-88996-669-2 (paperback)
ISBN: 979-8-88996-670-8 (ebook)

Editor: Alyssa Sorenson
Designer: Anna Peterson

Photo Credits: Nadia Yong/Shutterstock, cover; JIJI PRESS/AFP/Getty, 1; ChameleonsEye/Shutterstock, 3; Anton Balazh/Shutterstock, 4; Oskari Porkka/Shutterstock, 5; Avigator Fortuner/Shutterstock, 6; Antony Velikagathu/iStock, 7; Hum Images/Alamy, 8-9; Kip Evans/Alamy, 10-11; Kiser Photo Co. (Portland, Or.)/Oregon Historical Society Library, 12-13; University of Washington Libraries, Special Collections, Wilhelm Hester, photographer Hester10594, 13; Dee Browning/Shutterstock, 14-15; Ryan Tishken/iStock, 16-17; U.S. Navy/AP Images, 18-19; Conner Flecks/Alamy, 20; WaterFrame/Alamy, 21; David Pillow/Dreamstime, 23.

Printed in the United States of America at Corporate Graphics in North Mankato, Minnesota.

TABLE OF CONTENTS

CHAPTER 1

WELCOME TO THE PACIFIC OCEAN

The Pacific is the world's largest ocean. It touches North and South America. It goes all the way to Asia and Australia.

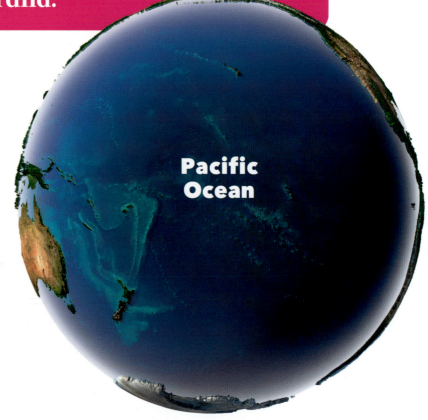

Pacific Ocean

Some areas of the Pacific are warm. Strong storms can start in warm water. This includes **hurricanes**. Ocean water in the north and south can be very cold. Ice and fog are dangerous.

CHAPTER 2

DANGEROUS WATERS AND WAR

People have sailed the Pacific Ocean for hundreds of years. Ships bring goods from one part of the world to another.

Ships in the Pacific can get caught in storms. They can crash into large rocks and hidden **reefs**.

Two Brothers's anchor

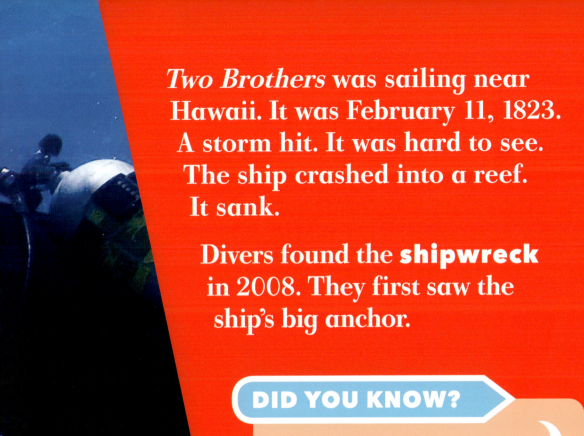

Two Brothers was sailing near Hawaii. It was February 11, 1823. A storm hit. It was hard to see. The ship crashed into a reef. It sank.

Divers found the **shipwreck** in 2008. They first saw the ship's big anchor.

DID YOU KNOW?

After *Two Brothers* sank, the **crew** held on to small **lifeboats** all night. Another ship **rescued** them in the morning.

In 1875, the SS *Pacific* was going to California. The ship had gold on it. Winds were strong. The ocean waves were rough. Another ship was nearby. They **collided**. The *Pacific* was **damaged**. It sunk.

A **remotely operated vehicle (ROV)** found the wreck in 2022. It was near Washington. As of 2023, people were still searching for the lost gold!

WHAT DO YOU THINK?

Shipwrecks are sometimes deep underwater. What tools would you use to find a shipwreck?

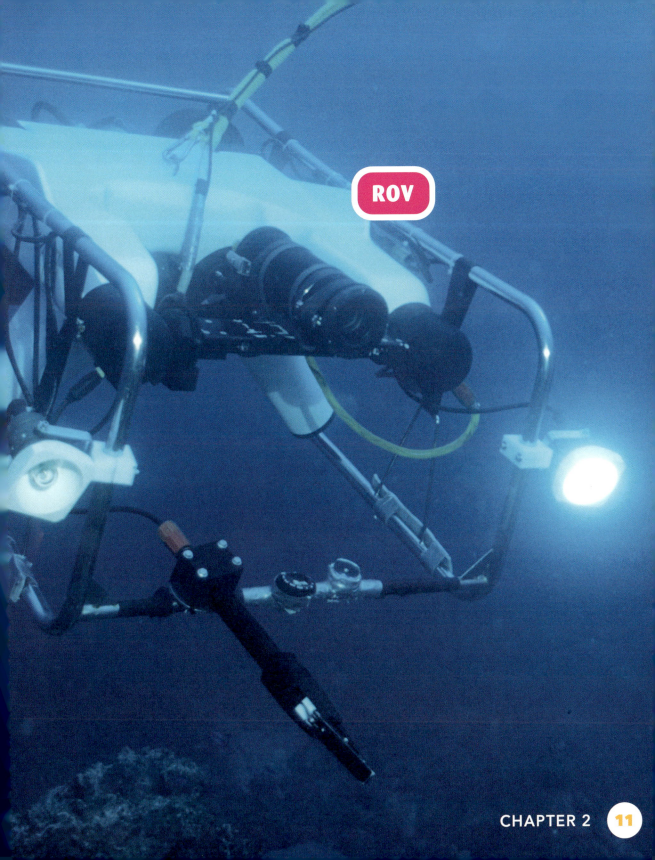

ROV

Peter Iredale

It was October 25, 1906. *Peter Iredale* was sailing to Oregon. It was close to shore. The wind picked up. A strong **current** pushed the ship onto the beach. Today, the shipwreck is still stuck in the sand.

Peter Iredale near shore

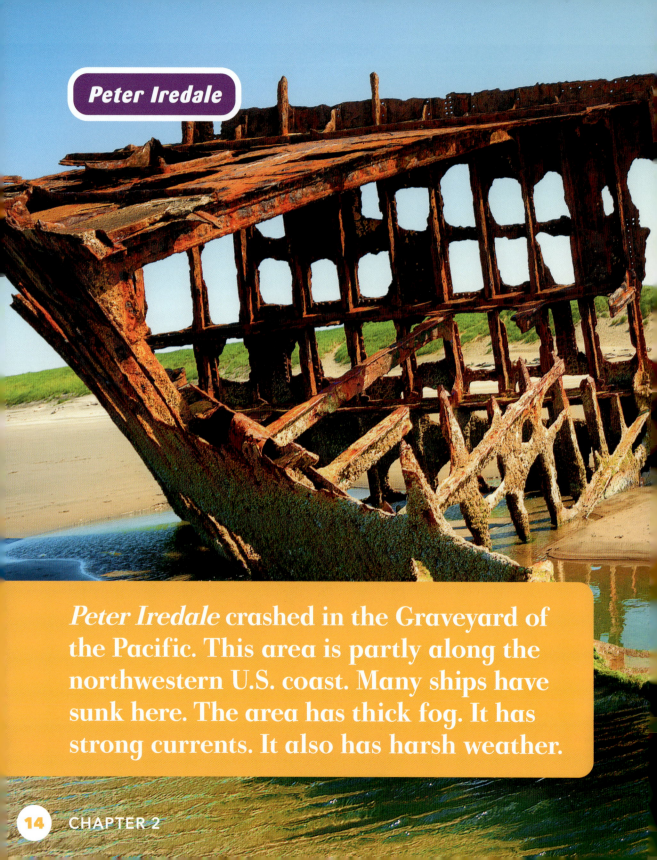

Peter Iredale crashed in the Graveyard of the Pacific. This area is partly along the northwestern U.S. coast. Many ships have sunk here. The area has thick fog. It has strong currents. It also has harsh weather.

TAKE A LOOK!

Where have ships sunk in the Graveyard of the Pacific along the U.S. coast? Take a look!

GRAVEYARD OF THE PACIFIC

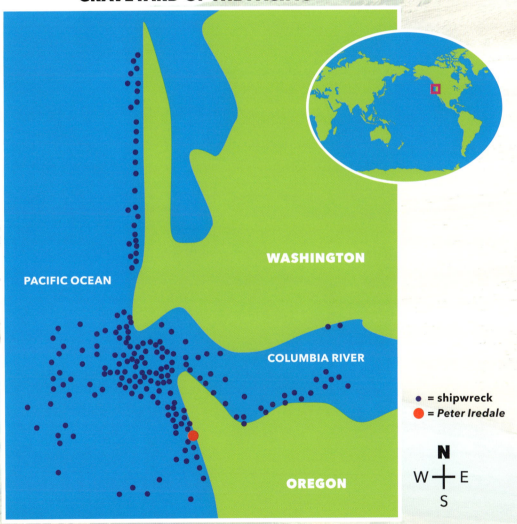

PACIFIC OCEAN

WASHINGTON

COLUMBIA RIVER

OREGON

- = shipwreck
- = *Peter Iredale*

N
W — E
S

USS *Arizona*
Memorial

USS VESTAL AR 4

USS ARIZONA BB 39

Arizona
shipwreck

The USS *Arizona* was a **battleship**. During **World War II** (1939–1945), it was in Pearl Harbor, Hawaii. On December 7, 1941, Japan dropped bombs there. The *Arizona* was hit. It exploded and sank. After the attack, the United States went to war against Japan.

WHAT DO YOU THINK?

In 1962, a **memorial** was made for the *Arizona*. It is in Pearl Harbor. People can see the shipwreck. Would you like to visit? Why or why not?

The USS *Hornet* was used in World War II. In October 1942, the United States and Japan battled at sea. Japan attacked the *Hornet*. It damaged the ship. U.S. ships saved most of the *Hornet*'s crew. Then Japan fired four **torpedoes**. The *Hornet* sank.

People found the shipwreck in 2019. It was 17,500 feet (5,335 meters) below the surface.

USS *Hornet*

CHAPTER 3

SAILING THE PACIFIC TODAY

Today's ships have more safety tools. Radios and **satellite phones** help crews communicate with people on land. Captains get weather updates at sea.

satellite phone

People search for shipwrecks in the Pacific Ocean. They use ROVs and other equipment to find and study them. What other wrecks are at the bottom of the ocean?

QUICK FACTS & TOOLS

WHERE THEY SANK IN THE PACIFIC

1. *Two Brothers* crashed into a reef near Hawaii on February 11, 1823. The wreck was found in 2008.

2. A ship crashed into the SS *Pacific* on November 4, 1875. *Pacific* sank near Cape Flattery in Washington.

3. In 1906, *Peter Iredale* crashed into Oregon's shore. The shipwreck is still in the sand today.

4. The USS *Arizona* was bombed on December 7, 1941. People can see the wreck today.

5. The USS *Hornet* sank on October 26, 1942. It was found in 2019.

GLOSSARY

battleship: A warship armed with powerful guns.

collided: Hit something violently.

crew: A group of people who work on a ship.

current: Water that moves in a specific direction.

damaged: Harmed.

hurricanes: Violent storms with heavy rain and high winds.

lifeboats: Boats on large ships that people use to get off the ships in emergencies.

memorial: A place or object made to remind people of something.

reefs: Strips of rocks, sand, or coral close to the surface of the ocean.

remotely operated vehicle (ROV): An unmanned underwater machine used to explore deep ocean water.

rescued: Saved from a dangerous situation.

satellite phones: Phones that can send and receive messages from satellites.

shipwreck: The remains of a sunken ship.

torpedoes: Missiles that can be launched underwater.

World War II: A war in which the United States, Australia, France, Great Britain, the Soviet Union, and other nations defeated Germany, Italy, and Japan.

INDEX

TO LEARN MORE

Finding more information is as easy as 1, 2, 3.

❶ Go to www.factsurfer.com

❷ Enter "PacificOceanshipwrecks" into the search box.

❸ Choose your book to see a list of websites.

FACT SURFER